For Edward

Composer's World

Claude Debussy

by Wendy Thompson

VIKING

Introduction

At first glance, the mainstream of Western music from the later Baroque period onwards seems to be firmly rooted in Central Europe. Bach, Haydn, Mozart, Beethoven, Schubert, Schumann, Brahms, Wagner, Mahler – all of them lived and worked in Germany or Austria. Not until the late nineteenth and early twentieth centuries did this great line of succession begin to branch out – with Tchaikovsky, Stravinsky, Rakhmaninov, Prokofiev, and Shostakovich emerging from Russia; Smetana, Dvořák, and Janáček from Bohemia; Bartók from Hungary; Elgar and Britten from England; Verdi from Italy; and from France, Ravel, Messiaen, and Boulez. And although French music has often been regarded as a pleasant diversion: charming, easy to listen to, but not really to be taken seriously, it was nevertheless a Frenchman, Claude Debussy, who broke the German monopoly in his search for a completely new sound-world. Although his output was relatively small, he freed music from the restraints of traditional forms – such as the symphony and sonata – in favor of pieces inspired by poems, moods, and landscapes; and by using unusual scales and harmonies to loosen the shackles of major and minor keys, Debussy paved the way for a vast range of experiments in twentieth-century music.

Debussy was born in a country with a politically unstable régime. Ever since the deposing of their King during the Revolution, the French had never seemed able to settle on any one form of government. They tried a quick succession of emperor/dictators and republics, and even restored the monarchy once or twice, but nothing seemed to work. When Debussy was still a child, the Second Empire of Napoleon III, under whose authoritarian rule France had

A scene from the Franco–Prussian War, 1870

prospered to become "the banker of the world," came to an abrupt end with the disastrous Franco-Prussian War. In a dispute over alliances and territory, France was humiliated by Germany and lost some of her lands. Finally, after a brief and unsuccessful attempt by the working classes to seize power (the Paris Commune), a Third Republic was set up, under a President – a system which has lasted ever since. But as the nineteenth century drew to its close, the great powers of Europe played a deadly game of chess on the board of the Western hemisphere, snapping up colonial pawns wherever they could. Empires expanded rapidly: the British in India, the Far East, Australia and Canada, and the French on the African continent and in Indochina. Meanwhile Germany concentrated on building up her armaments, and strengthening her economic and military might, dangerously close to the borders of her old enemy, France. The war machine that was to shatter European civilization in 1914 was already primed.

While the politicians played their power games, the arts flourished. Thanks to the architect Baron Haussmann, who replaced ancient, tangled slums with magnificent new houses and apartment blocks flanking wide, straight, tree-lined

Above right: The poet Charles Baudelaire (1821–1867)
Below right: The poet Stéphane Mallarmé (1842–1898)

boulevards, Paris became not only the world's most elegant, cosmopolitan city, but also the artistic hub of Europe. During a period known as the "Belle Epoque" – the Beautiful Era – the city positively bubbled over with talent. In a heady atmosphere of pleasure, great wealth rubbed shoulders with dire poverty, but writers, poets, and musicians felt free to be original and creative. While the refined Marcel Proust struggled to capture the essence of a passing era, novelists such as Maupassant and Zola shocked readers by their vivid descriptions of real life in gilded mansions or squalid gutters. In literary salons a whole generation of poets – among them Verlaine, Baudelaire, and Mallarmé – tried to find new means of expressing their thoughts through the symbolic power of words. And in the garrets of Montmartre, a concentration of brilliant painters – whose canvases, which were often sold then for a few francs or exchanged for a meal, now fetch astronomical prices –

astonished conservative art-lovers with a bewildering range of new techniques: Monet's "impressions" of sunlit waterlilies and haystacks, Renoir's opulent Parisian women; Degas' studies of racehorses and ballet dancers; Seurat's "pointillist" landscapes, made up of tiny dots of color; the powerful, "primitive" art of van Gogh and Gauguin; Toulouse-Lautrec's vivid scenes of Parisian nightlife and the underworld; the young Picasso's sad clowns.

But French music, then still dominated by German taste and training, lagged behind; and it took Debussy's genius to absorb all these influences and apply them to his own unique art – French in its subtle, sensuous charm, but universal in its bold originality. "Composers aren't daring enough," he once complained. "Music is freer than perhaps any other art-form, since it doesn't have to try to reproduce Nature exactly, but is able to explore the mysterious relationship between Nature and Imagination."

Second Empire Paris: the Champs-Elysées

Debussy aged 5

1 Childhood

Claude-Achille Debussy was born on August 22, 1862, in the Parisian suburb of Saint-Germain-en-Laye. His parents, Manuel and Victorine, rented a small china shop, but the business did not thrive. By the time Claude was five, the family had moved to the center of Paris. Manuel Debussy flitted from job to job; first he worked as a travelling salesman, then at a printer's, and then as a junior clerk; but he really wanted to be a soldier. In 1870 he realized his ambition: France went to war with Germany, and Manuel joined the National Guard. A year later he became a captain in the revolutionary forces of the Paris Commune. In the spring of 1871, the "Communards" tried to seize political power, but the uprising was savagely suppressed, and 30,000 Frenchmen died at the hands of their own country-men. Manuel Debussy was tried and sentenced to a year's imprisonment – something which his son later tried to cover up and never spoke about.

Street fighting at a barricade during the Paris Commune

Manuel-Achille Debussy, the composer's father

Victorine Debussy, the composer's mother

Victorine Debussy apparently disliked small children, and took little notice of her own brood. Claude and his three surviving brothers and sisters were often packed off to their aunt Clémentine in Cannes. She encouraged young Claude to start playing the piano; and when he went back to Paris, he continued his lessons. One of his first teachers there was Madame Mauté de Fleurville, a former pupil of Chopin. She recognized that the boy had talent, and persuaded Manuel Debussy – who was determined that his eldest son should become a sailor – to allow Claude to take his musical studies further. Visions of untold wealth to be earned from his son's career as a great virtuoso unfolded before Manuel's greedy eyes, and so, at the age of ten, in October 1872, Claude passed the highly competitive entrance examination admitting him to the Paris Conservatoire.

This great institution, founded during the French Revolution, was the main French training school for players and composers. But it had a reputation for conservatism, and while many of its successful students ended up as very second-rate musicians, the most naturally gifted were often overlooked or discouraged because they failed to conform. In later life, Debussy remembered the Conservatoire as that "gloomy, dirty place where the dust of bad habits clings to one's fingers." But he was lucky to be taught piano by Antoine Marmontel, a bald-headed little man with a long pointed beard, whose own career as a virtuoso had long been forgotten – if indeed it had ever existed. At any rate, as his students quickly discovered, Marmontel could hardly play the piano at all, but loved teaching music. The composer Bizet once declared that in Marmontel's class, "you learn something more than the piano; you learn how to become a musician."

Under Marmontel's supervision, Claude made quick progress. His performance of Chopin's Second Piano Concerto at the age of eleven won him a certificate of merit; and a year later he was described as a "twelve-year-old prodigy who promises to be a first-rate virtuoso." But before long, his rebellious temperament began to assert itself. Instead of diligently practicing his studies and pieces, he preferred either to play arrangements of quartets by Mozart and Haydn, or to try out intriguing new combinations of chords and arpeggios. "What rule do you follow?" asked a suspicious professor. "My own pleasure!" declared Claude. By the time he was fourteen, his playing had become "irresponsible

Debussy as a Conservatoire student, aged about 12

Paris: the Seine today

and muddle-headed," according to his bewildered teacher, and over the next two years he won no piano prizes at all. He did, however, walk away with plenty of theory prizes. He also took a few lessons from the great organist and composer César Franck – although he found Franck's teaching methods too severe. "Modulate, modulate!" Franck is supposed to have cried. "Why should I?" replied Claude. "I'm quite happy with the key I'm playing in."

Since money was tight at home, Debussy also began to take a series of summer jobs, playing chamber music to entertain wealthy aristocrats. In 1879 he spent a few months at Chenonceaux, one of the loveliest castles in the Loire valley, where his main job was to lull the mistress of the house to sleep by playing soothing music in the early hours of the morning. The following year, he joined the household of the Russian multi-millionairess Madame von Meck, Tchaikovsky's patron. Over the next three years, Debussy spent every summer travelling all over Europe and Russia with the large von Meck family. He was expected to give piano and theory lessons to the younger children, and to play in a piano trio: among the pieces they played in 1882 was a new trio by Tchaikovsky. Madame von Meck genuinely looked forward to Debussy's annual visits. "Now I shall have lots of music, and he livens up the whole house," she wrote to Tchaikovsky in August 1882. "He's a real Parisian, witty, and a wonderful mimic . . . he's so good-humored and has a charming nature." "Our nervous, gay, thin little Frenchman cheers up our solemn household no end," reported her thirteen-year-old daughter Sonia, with whom Debussy flirted shamelessly. Meanwhile, he was fascinated by the colorful, vivid music of the nationalist Russians – Borodin, Balakirev, Musorgsky, Rimsky-Korsakov – and Tchaikovsky in particular. Madame von Meck sent some of Debussy's own early compositions (including a symphony in the distinctly Russian key of B minor) to Tchaikovsky, who returned them with valuable comments. This passion for Russian music stayed with Debussy, and perhaps influenced his own later technique of writing music in short, repetitive phrases rather than full-blown melodies. Ever receptive to atmosphere, he savored his Russian experiences; and when the time came to leave the luxurious splendor of Madame von Meck's mansions and return to his parents' wretched little attic flat in the run-down Parisian district of Montmartre, he "wept like a child."

César Franck (1822–1890)

*Madame von Meck's piano trio:
Debussy is on the right*

2 Rome

On Christmas Eve 1880, the eighteen-year-old Debussy began to take formal composition lessons at the Conservatoire with the genial Ernest Guiraud. Although Guiraud found this shy, awkward young man "clumsy and strange" at first, a warm friendship soon developed between master and pupil, and the two spent long afternoons together discussing musical problems, or playing billiards. Success at the Conservatoire, however, depended on academic awards and prizes, and Debussy found himself being pulled in two different directions. On the one hand, he really wanted to sit at the piano all day, trying out all sorts of new combinations of sounds, from "chromatic groanings imitating the buses going down the street" to shimmering sequences of arpeggios streaming down the keyboard like rain. On the other, he had to force himself to work through boring fugues and other exercises to please his teachers, who thought him a dangerous fanatic.

In 1883 Debussy entered for the Prix de Rome competition. Competitors for this famous prize, awarded by the French Academy of Fine Arts, had to take a difficult examination behind locked doors. In addition to exercises in fugue and counterpoint, candidates had to set to music a specially written text (usually about heroic or mythical characters from Ancient Greece or Rome). The winner was then packed off to Rome, where he (or, eventually, she) could stay for up to four years at the imposing Villa Medici. Apart from being expected to send regular compositions back to Paris, the lucky prizewinner could then improve his general education by travelling around Italy, studying its art, music, and literature. Unfortunately, the judges of the competition were often very old, very conservative, and half-deaf, so the prize frequently went to the wrong person.

1883-1887

A photograph of Debussy taken in Rome

Debussy won second prize in 1883. The following year he re-entered with his cantata *L'enfant prodigue* (The Prodigal Son). "I was standing on the Pont des Arts," he later recalled, "fascinated by the exquisite play of the sunlight on the rippling water . . . Suddenly, someone tapped me on the shoulder and said breathlessly, 'You've won!' No one would believe me, but in that moment all my joy was over . . . I felt that I was no longer free."

There was a good reason for this strange reaction. For the past two years or so, Debussy had been having an affair with the young wife of a building contractor, an amateur singer called Madame Vasnier. The Vasniers had shown

this horrible Villa," he wrote to Monsieur Vasnier. "The weather is dreadful – wind and rain. You must admit that it seems pointless to have left Paris . . ." Debussy found his fellow prizewinners boring and conceited; the Director was a "jailer," and he hated his room – a huge, dark cavern of a place known as the "Etruscan Tomb." In the two miserable years he spent there, he managed to finish only two pieces to send back to Paris. The second of these, an orchestral suite called *Printemps* (Spring), is still played today. Debussy described it as a "work of a special color, re-creating as many feelings as possible from the point of view of living things . . . I wanted to express the slow, laborious birth of natural things, and finally a burst of joy at being reborn." Even so, Debussy could not be bothered to finish the work: he sent it off to Paris in a version for piano, and pretended that the full orchestral score had been burnt at the binders. With unusual foresight, the judges at the Academy criticized the work's "vague impressionism."

By February 1887, Debussy had had enough of Rome. The one highlight was meeting the great pianist and composer Liszt: thirty years later he recalled how Liszt had made the piano "breathe" by his sensitive use of the pedal. Other than that, Debussy's stay in Rome had been a "wasted experience that has merely set me back." During his second year there he had already run back to Paris three times. Now he left for good.

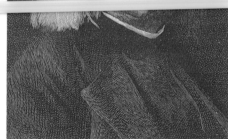

Franz Liszt (1811–1886)

great kindness to the penniless young student, and invited him often to their home. A strong attachment had grown up between the blonde, green-eyed Marie-Adélaide, and the dark, handsome Debussy, whose Renaissance hairstyle and neatly trimmed beard led to his friends calling him "The Prince of Darkness." Debussy accompanied Madame Vasnier at private recitals, and wrote several songs for her. She was the first of many women in his life, and their "mad, blinding love" lasted for several years. No one knows whether Monsieur Vasnier was aware of the situation, but when Debussy showed great reluctance to take up his Rome prize, Vasnier certainly did everything he could to persuade him to go.

So at the age of twenty-two, in the middle of winter, D........... .... Already homesick by the time he reached Marseilles, he arrived in Rome determined to hate everything about it. "Here I am in

A scene from "Lohengrin"

3 From Wagner to Symbolism

Debussy's homecoming was far from happy. His father had lost his job, and both parents bitterly reproached their son for failing to live up to his early promise and, in particular, for not bringing in any money. Furthermore, he found that two years' separation had altered Madame Vasnier's feelings for him, and within a few months their relationship had been broken off. With time on his hands, Debussy rediscovered the joys of Parisian life, sauntering along the "quais" of the Seine, rummaging in bookstalls, and sitting for hours in cafés where he listened to artists and writers discussing art, life, love, and politics. One of his favorite places was the Bookshop of Independent Art. Its owner, the publisher Edmond Bailly, introduced Debussy to the latest literature, especially the works of the group of poets known as the "Symbolists."

In 1887, the French conductor Charles Lamoureux put on a performance of Wagner's opera *Lohengrin* in Paris. Unfortunately, the bitter memories of the Franco-Prussian war still rankled: Wagner's music was hissed at by the French audience, and the opera had to be hastily withdrawn. But Debussy was bowled over by Wagner's grandiose idea of "music-drama." The following year he set out for Bayreuth, the German town north of Nuremberg where Wagner had built a special "Festival Playhouse" exclusively for the performances of his own operas. There, along with other "pilgrims," including Hugo Wolf and Gustav Mahler, Debussy heard *Parsifal* and *The Mastersingers of Nurem-*

The Wagner Festspielhaus at Bayreuth

A view of Paris today

berg. Nowadays the idea of the music festival is common-place, but in the 1880s it was quite new. Although accommodations were ridiculously expensive, the food dreadful, and the seats at the opera house itself hard and uncomfortable, thousands of visitors flocked to hear the works of the Master, who inspired the same kind of hysterical devotion as today's pop stars. Wagner's music struck Debussy like a blinding revelation. The following summer he returned to Bayreuth, where he heard *Tristan and Isolde* for the first time. Although he was soon to rebel against the powerful seduction of the "old poisoner," Debussy never really shook off Wagner's influence: twenty-six years later he literally quaked with emotion after hearing a performance of *Tristan*. Many of his later works were haunted by "the ghost of old Klingsor" (the magician in *Parsifal*); but it was hardly surprising that his own attempt at writing a grand opera on Wagnerian lines, a heroic tale of love, death, and chivalry set in medieval Spain, ended in disillusionment. After struggling through three acts of *Rodrigue et Chimène*, Debussy gave up in despair and pretended to his friends that the table on which he had been working had accidentally overturned, conveniently dumping the manuscript into the fire.

Meanwhile, he was moving towards a new musical language, a music that should be "flexible, and adaptable to fantasies and dreams." So far, he had written about forty songs, mostly to elusive, whimsical texts by contemporary French poets. Now, six of his settings of Symbolist poems by Paul Verlaine were published as a set, called *Ariettes, paysages belges et aquarelles* (Little Songs, Belgian Land-scapes and Watercolors). Led by Mallarmé, the Symbolists relied heavily on the particular sound and color of the French language rather than on the literal meaning of words. Many of their verses are practically impossible to translate,

although titles such as "*C'est l'extase*" (This Is Ecstasy), "*Chevaux de bois*" (Wooden Horses), and "*Il pleure dans mon coeur*" (It Rains in My Heart) give some idea of what the poem is supposed to be about. This art of allusion, often tinged with morbid, decadent imagery, appealed greatly to Debussy. At the same time, he began to transcribe some new, experimental piano sounds into notes on paper. One of the ways he found to free his music from the straitjacket of conventional harmony was to use a scale based on whole tones, without the semitones which force a piece into a definite "tonality" or key. The whole-tone harmonics give his music its distinctive blurred, sonorous effect. The first fruit of his efforts was a pair of delicate *Arabesques*, effective, and quite easy to play; and *Petite Suite* for piano duet.

Richard Wagner (1813–1883)

"En bâteau" from the "Petite Suite"

11

Javanese dancers at the Paris Exhibition, 1889

In 1889 Paris celebrated the centenary of the Revolution with a spectacular World Fair. Its greatest attraction was the specially built Eiffel Tower, then the world's tallest building. The tower was meant to be only a temporary structure, but it was never dismantled, and its gaunt skeleton has since become the most famous landmark in Paris. Debussy, however, could not tear himself away from the Javanese pavilion. Here, for the first time, he heard an entirely new kind of music. Brilliantly clad dancers, their heads crowned by garlands of flowers, wove graceful patterns to the accompaniment of an exotic "gamelan" orchestra of delicate percussion instruments – tuned gongs, bells, xylophones, and tiny cymbals creating "endless combinations of ethereal, flashing timbres." Compared with the subtle economy of this hypnotic Oriental music based on five-note, or "pentatonic," scales, Western percussion instru-

ments sounded like "rustic noises at a country fair." Furthermore, Debussy realized that it did not necessarily take a massive orchestra and an overblown soprano to make a striking effect: "A shrill little clarinet can set the mood, and a gong can create a sense of terror."

The World Fair also offered a unique display of decorative arts and objects from all over the world. Ever since his glimpse of wealth and luxury at Madame von Meck's, Debussy had loved beautiful things, especially fragile, exquisitely painted porcelain vases and delicate Oriental paintings. "Desire is everything," he wrote to a friend. "One longs madly but sincerely for a work of art, whether it's a Velasquez painting, a Satsuma vase, or a new tie. How wonderful to own it. This is real love." As well as these, the exhibition was full of "Art Nouveau" (New Art), a movement closely related to Symbolist literature. Characterized by swirling lines, bold designs based on peacock feathers, orchids, and lilies, and by depictions of pale girls dressed in

Decorative Art Nouveau entrance to a Métro station

13

flowing robes with long, wavy blonde hair, Art Nouveau was itself highly symbolic. The nineteenth century, which had brought huge changes to people's lives with its emphasis on practical matters, especially industrial and technological progress, was drawing to a close; and among artists in particular, there was a sense of decay, of the end of an era. People no longer looked forward with confidence, sure of a world which would inevitably get better. Instead they turned for comfort and inspiration to a mythical, nostalgic past which actually never existed – a world of knights, Botticelli-like maidens, and fantastic flowers and vegetation, all symbols of love and death.

Debussy's own musical piece of Art Nouveau was completed around this time. *La damoiselle élue* (The Blessed Damozel), based on a poem by the English Pre-Raphaelite artist and poet Dante Gabriel Rossetti, uses swirling arabesques of melody, accompanied by an unusual palette of orchestral tone-color to depict the Damozel herself, "leaning over the golden bar of heaven." The work was published four years later by Edmond Bailly in a special limited edition, at the same time as Oscar Wilde's scandalously decadent play *Salome*.

Oscar Wilde (1854–1900)

Gabrielle Dupont, Debussy's girlfriend, 1892–8

Women at a Cafe, Evening, by Degas (1877)

4 The Bohemian Years

Some time in the early 1890s Debussy met a green-eyed girl from Normandy, named Gabrielle Dupont. Gaby, as she was known, had no actual profession: she was one of thousands of country girls who came up to Paris every year, hoping to make their fortunes. While England, under the gloomy rule of its widowed Queen, took a sternly moralistic view of such matters, Paris in the last years of the nineteenth century was known all over Europe as a city for lovers. Frenchmen considered it quite natural to have both a wife and a mistress; and foreigners in all walks of life, from England's own Prince of Wales downwards, knew that they could always find pretty girls in Paris. It was still rare for a respectable woman to have a proper job other than marriage, and many girls from poor backgrounds could only make a living by selling themselves. Some even mapped out their prospective careers: by a series of affairs with men, rising ever higher up the social scale, they dreamed of

achieving the heights reached by a select few. These legendary "grandes horizontales," such as Caroline Otero, Liane de Pougy, and Hortense Schneider, could ask thousands of francs for a single night, and chose their lovers from among Europe's richest and most powerful men. At the other end of the scale were the streetwalkers, who eked out a miserable living in the Parisian gutters. Clearly it was better to start somewhere in between, perhaps through a love affair with an artist. Debussy and Gaby were to share a life of poverty, living in a garret for seven years or so, until he began to fret for marriage and respectability and she finally tired of his chronic lack of money. Yet in some ways, their years together were to be Debussy's happiest: "It was no life of luxury, but even so, it was the best time of all."

The only place where Debussy could afford a room of his own was in the Montmartre district, a ramshackle, working-class village crawling up the "Butte" or hill. In the

15

277. - PARIS (18e). - Moulin de la Galette
(Date de 1295)   J. H.

The Moulin de la Galette, Montmartre

1890s the great, white basilica of Sacré-Coeur, which now dominates the Montmartre skyline, had not yet been completed, and the hill was covered with orchards, vineyards, and picturesque windmills. Since 1871, the district had become the focus for artists, poets, and musicians who enjoyed a "Bohemian" lifestyle – sitting at cheap wooden tables outside the smoky little cafés and brasseries around the Place du Tertre, drinking rough red wine, chasing girls – and at night, hanging round the many nightclubs and music halls which flourished around the Place Pigalle. Now rather squalid and tourist-ridden, this famous square was then lined with artists' studios, and with cafés such as Weber's, where the finest minds of the time discussed art, literature, philosophy, and politics; and the Irish-American bar Reynold's, a favorite haunt of the racing world, where the Irish

Inside a Parisian music-hall

Dancing the can-can at Les Ambassadeurs night-club

singer May Belfort dressed up as a little girl to sing "Daddy wouldn't buy me a bow-wow" in a highly suggestive way. Debussy found the atmosphere at Reynold's "very aesthetic!"

In 1889 the famous Moulin Rouge (Red Windmill) opened in Pigalle, and people of all social classes, among them Claude and Gaby, flocked to see artists such as Yvette Guilbert, Jane Avril, and "La Goulue" singing their throaty, wistful songs about love and separation, or dancing the can-can (with or without underwear!) to Offenbach's hectic music. The atmosphere of this vibrant, noisy, colorful world of the night is captured forever in the pictures of Toulouse-Lautrec, just one of the many painters who found inspira-

tion in Montmartre. A few doors away, the New Circus offered a variety of acts including the English clown Footitt and his Moorish companion Chocolat; while for those seeking rather more upmarket entertainment, there was the Chat Noir (Black Cat) nightclub, decorated with skeletons and other grotesque symbols, whose proprietor made a habit of deliberately insulting everyone who walked through its doors. The Chat Noir was made famous in a song by the flamboyant entertainer Aristide Bruant:

> I seek my fortune
> around the Black Cat
> on a moonlit evening
> in Montmartre.

It was in this lively, stimulating atmosphere that Debussy struggled to create a new sound-world: one of subtle, shifting harmonies, fragments of melodies that flicker through gossamer veils like pinpoints of light, capturing on paper the essence of a breath of wind, the rustle of leaves, a shaft of moonlight on a rooftop. Sometimes he turned for inspiration to an elusive dream-world of the past, peopled by mocking ghosts, Harlequins and their Columbines masked in pale silks, playing mandolins and guitars or dancing to plaintive sarabands. These visions came to life in pieces such as the *Suite bergamasque* for piano, whose third piece is the haunting *Clair de lune* (Moonlight) – considered so dangerously alluring that straitlaced Parisian matrons forbade their daughters to learn it – and in songs based on Verlaine's evocative poetry, such as the first set of *Fêtes galantes* (Romantic Celebrations); three songs about love called "Softly," "Puppets," and "Moonlight."

*Chocolat dancing at the Bar d'Achille, 1896,
by Toulouse-Lautrec.*

18

"Clair de lune" from the "Suite bergamasque"

19

20

the best claret. Once, when Debussy criticized Satie's music for having no form, Satie simply shrugged his shoulders and responded with "Three Pieces in the Form of a Pear"; and while Debussy's piano music carries instructions such as "further away," or "in a shimmering haze," Satie's instructs the player to "slow down politely," and "play like a nightingale with toothache."

Another friend in Debussy's Bohemian period was the composer Ernest Chausson, a wealthy and cultured man who entertained at his sumptuous Paris home all the greatest talents of the time: artists such as Renoir, Manet, Degas, and Rodin; writers such as André Gide, Mallarmé, the notorious music critic Monsieur Willy and his child-wife, Colette; and musicians – Franck, Fauré, and d'Indy, as well as younger unknowns including Debussy and Satie. It was perhaps Chausson who urged Debussy to write his only string quartet. Unlike his other music of the time, the String Quartet is a piece of "pure music": it has no literary or

Among Debussy's acquaintances at the Chat Noir was an eccentric young man named Erik Satie, who played the piano in nightclubs for a living. The self-styled "official musician" to a bizarre and rather sinister semi-religious sect called the Rosicrucians (in which Debussy was also reputed to have been deeply involved), Satie was himself a Harlequin figure, who hid his naturally gentle and rather melancholy temperament under a clown's mask of acid wit and self-mockery. His eccentric habits – such as buying twelve identical grey velvet suits – soon made him notorious; while his own piano pieces, written in a sparse, almost primitive style, carried bizarre titles such as *Gymnopédies* and *Gnossiennes* – no one really knew what they were supposed to mean. Satie quickly recognized Debussy's genius. For twenty-five years he remained a close friend and admirer, even though Debussy often snubbed him – in later years when Satie came to dinner, Debussy would put out a cheap bottle of wine for his old friend, while he and his wife drank

Debussy playing at the Chaussons' home in Luzancy, 1893

pictorial associations, but the movements are linked together by variants of the same musical material – a device which Chausson's teacher César Franck used in many of his compositions. The Quartet was a great success when it was first performed at the end of 1893 by the Belgian violinist Eugène Ysaÿe and his colleagues: one critic wrote that Debussy was "rotten with talent." The friendship, however, didn't last. Chausson belonged to respectable middle-class circles – and when Debussy went to visit him, Gaby had to be left at home. In 1894 Debussy met a friend of the Chaussons, a young singer called Thérèse Roger. He proposed marriage – but the engagement was quickly broken off "in unpleasant circumstances" (probably Thérèse found out about Gaby, who refused to be simply "dismissed"). Chausson was furious and never forgave Debussy.

At much the same time, Debussy was working on the piece which was to make his name. For some time, he had been a regular visitor to the famous Tuesday evening sessions which the poet Mallarmé held at his house in the rue de Rome. One of Mallarmé's best-known poems was "*L'après-midi d'un faune*" (The Afternoon of a Faun), an erotic monologue intended to be read out loud on stage. It describes a faun (a mythological figure, part-goat, part-human) lying in the long grass on a hot afternoon in ancient Greece, dreaming lazily of making love to two beautiful nymphs. Debussy's *Prélude à l'après-midi d'un faune*, completed in 1894, opened up a new world of orchestral sound. From the first languorous notes of the Faun's flute, it weaves a tantalizing veil of colors and textures, mirroring the Faun's fleeting dreams and desires. "You learn more about orchestration by listening to leaves blowing in the wind than by studying treatises," said Debussy; and he dispensed with noisy brass instruments in favor of the sensuous effect created by a rich combination of woodwinds, two harps,

and a pair of tiny antique cymbals. Debussy first played the piece through on the piano to Mallarmé, who arrived looking "like an old fortune-teller, with a Scotch plaid over his shoulders." The poet listened in silence; after a long pause, he said: "I didn't expect anything like this. It is music that brings out the feeling in my poem, conjuring up the atmosphere better than any color." Later, he sent Debussy a copy of the poem, inscribed:

> If you would know with what sweet harmonies
> Your flute resounds, O god of the woods,
> Then pay attention to the light
> With which Debussy infuses it.

Although the first performance on December 22, 1894, was spoilt by poor orchestral playing, the Prelude – now one of Debussy's most popular works – was a triumph. "From that moment," wrote Pierre Boulez many years later, "music began to beat with a new pulse."

1891-1896

The opening of "L'après-midi d'un faune"

23

A scene from an early production of "Pelléas et Mélisande"

Encouraged by the success of the "Faun," Debussy went on to finish the other major work of his Bohemian years. In 1893 he had begun an opera based on a play by Maurice Maeterlinck, a Belgian Symbolist playwright. *Pelléas et Mélisande* is set in the mists of time, in an allegorical kingdom called Allemonde. The young, innocent Mélisande has been persuaded to marry a middle-aged prince named Golaud. He carries her off to his ancient,

Maurice Maeterlinck (1862–1949)

gloomy castle, where she meets his younger half-brother, Pelléas. The two fall in love; but when Golaud finds out he kills Pelléas. Mélisande gives birth to a daughter and dies. The remarkable thing about the play is that hardly anything happens: the characters seem to have no motivation, but passively accept their fate. Debussy became deeply involved with "these two poor little things," as he called them. Mélisande – a typically Art Nouveau heroine, pale, fragile, with long thick fair hair – especially seemed to come alive in his imagination. "It is Mélisande's fault," he wrote to Chausson, "so please forgive us both. I have spent days chasing that 'empty air' that she is made of."

Debussy finished *Pelléas et Mélisande* in 1895, but it was seven years before it reached the stage. Even then, the première at the Opéra-Comique on April 30, 1902, was almost ruined by a violent quarrel between Debussy and Maeterlinck, apparently because the poet objected to the choice of singer for Mélisande (he wanted his own mistress to take the role). Poet and composer almost came to blows, and Maeterlinck washed his hands of the whole business, declaring that he hoped it would be a "resounding failure." It nearly was. Few people understood the poetic mastery of Debussy's score, in which he uses silence as "perhaps the only way of throwing the emotional weight of a phrase into relief." The public was noisily hostile; some of Debussy's most ardent supporters were puzzled; the Director of the Conservatoire forbade his students to see it, and the critics did not know what to make of it. "This music overwhelms you, drives deep into your heart with an inspired power that I admire but can't completely understand," wrote one. Though he toyed for years with other operatic subjects, especially Edgar Allan Poe's Gothic horror story "The Fall of the House of Usher," Debussy never finished another opera. *Pelléas* remains a unique masterpiece.

447. – PARIS – Opéra-Comique   *J. H*

The Opéra-Comique, Paris, where
"Pelléas" was first performed

5 Marriage

Pierre Louÿs at his harmonium

After Debussy's brief engagement to Thérèse Roger, he and Gaby resumed their often stormy relationship. But fidelity was not one of Debussy's strong points, and in 1897 another crisis flared up. "I've been mixed up in a horrid business," Debussy wrote to his friend, the poet Pierre Louÿs. "Gaby-of-the-steely-eyes found a letter in my pocket which left no doubt as to the advanced state of a love affair, full of the most picturesque details . . . whereupon tears, scenes, a real revolver . . . it's like something out of the gutter press. It's all stupid, and it changes nothing: you can't wipe out kisses and caresses with an india-rubber. That would be a good invention – the Adulterer's India-Rubber!" In fact, Gaby had tried to shoot herself, but was not seriously hurt.

Debussy had met the handsome and talented Pierre Louÿs, eight years younger than he, in 1893. "Among my friends you are definitely the one I have loved best," wrote Debussy. The two shared many similar tastes, in music, literature, and women. Louÿs was a colorful character: when he was twenty-one, his doctor told him that he probably had only three years to live. He promptly set about squandering his fortune, judging that he and the money would run out together. But things did not go according to plan, and on Christmas Eve, 1894, Louÿs found himself very much alive, but totally broke. He then turned his hand to writing mildly pornographic novels, and two years later his *Aphrodite* proved a best-seller. Attracted by exotic delights, Louÿs often visited North Africa, and brought back a succession of young Arab mistresses, who shared his home until he got bored and sent them back. Between 1897 and 1898 Debussy worked on a set of three songs based on poems by Louÿs, entitled *Chansons de Bilitis* (Songs of

Debussy photographed by Pierre Louÿs

Bilitis). Bilitis is an imaginary young girl in ancient Greece (a distant "mythical" setting was thought less likely to cause offense), who recalls her meetings with her lover. Debussy's music perfectly reflects the languid passion of the poems.

For the past few years, Debussy had eked out a meager living from giving piano lessons (which he hated), and borrowing from richer friends, such as Louÿs. From 1894 until 1900 he enjoyed the support of a generous publisher named Georges Hartmann, who gave him an annual income of 6000 francs a year. "He was sent to me by Providence," declared the composer, who still found himself penniless. This was partly due to the fact that whenever he had money in his pocket he would go out and buy himself some beautiful, expensive object that had caught his eye, such as a silk tie, or a Japanese print. Poor Gaby had to try to manage the housekeeping on next to nothing, in the squalid little attic room she and Debussy shared. Always untidy, the room contained little but a rickety table, three cane chairs, a makeshift bed, and a fine Pleyel piano – on loan!

While Debussy tried to finish another orchestral piece, the couple were quarrelling almost constantly. In March 1898 he wrote to Louÿs: "The three *Nocturnes* have been infected by my private life, first hopeful, then despairing, then just nothing! I've never been able to work when I'm going through a crisis . . . people who say they can write masterpieces in floods of tears are just hypocrites." The *Nocturnes* were finally finished a year later. The first, *Nuages* (Clouds), was inspired by the Seine on a grey day: Debussy uses a cor anglais (a low oboe) to imitate the sound of a pleasure-boat's hooter. *Fêtes* (Festivals) brilliantly evokes a carnival atmosphere, complete with brass band; while *Sirènes* (Sirens) is a delicate seascape, in which a women's chorus, singing without words, suggests the mer-

Festival Day, by Monet

maids who lure sailors to their doom. As painters such as Monet abandoned bold outlines and a literal approach in favor of freer brushstrokes which created the impression of a shaft of light here, a shadow there, so Debussy's music had by then come to be associated with this "impressionist" technique. Through fluid harmonies based on whole-tone or pentatonic scales, short, repetitive melodic motifs rather than finished melodies, and freedom of form rather than clearly defined musical structures, he too was able to capture in music a fleeting moment of light or shade, a ripple of water, a passing cloud.

Just as he finished the *Nocturnes*, Debussy's relationship with Gaby finally came to an end. "Life has been quite full lately," he wrote to Georges Hartmann. "I've moved house, and Mlle Dupont, my 'secretary,' has resigned. It's been very upsetting . . ." When asked many years later what life with Debussy had been like, Gaby replied, "We had many rows owing to lack of money." On leaving him, she resumed her "career" and became an aristocrat's mistress, although her good fortune did not last, and she died in great poverty at the end of the Second World War. Despite their arguments, Debussy always remembered her with affection. In 1902 he sent her a copy of *Pelléas*, inscribed: "To Gaby, princess of the mysterious kingdom of Allemonde. Her faithful old Claude Debussy."

It was not only Debussy's private life that was undergoing a tempestuous upheaval at the time. In 1898 the writer Émile Zola issued his famous pamphlet *J'accuse!*, and plunged France into one of the greatest political scandals of all time. Four years earlier a French army officer named Alfred Dreyfus had been tried and condemned by a military tribunal to life imprisonment for allegedly spying for the Germans. Dreyfus was Jewish, and many people believed

Le Petit Journal
CHAQUE JOUR 5 CENTIMES
Le Supplément illustré
CHAQUE SEMAINE 5 CENTIMES

Le Petit Journal

SUPPLÉMENT ILLUSTRÉ

ABONNEMENTS

Huit pages : CINQ centimes

Sixième année   DIMANCHE 13 JANVIER 1895   Numero 2

LE TRAITRE
Dégradation d'Alfred Dreyfus

Alfred Dreyfus is publicly dishonored

that he was innocent, but had been framed by his anti-Jewish fellow officers. The Dreyfus Affair, as it became known, split the country into the liberal supporters of Dreyfus, and the Establishment – the government and the army – whom Zola accused of covering up the truth. Dreyfus spent five years in the dreaded prison camp on Devil's Island before it finally became known that the documents which convicted him had been forged. He came back, a broken man, to a state pardon, while the French officer who really had been guilty committed suicide. But the Dreyfus Affair was not so easily laid to rest: it had stirred up a hornet's nest of nationalist, anti-Jewish feelings in France, and from then on the Socialist government, under a quick succession of prime ministers, struggled to stem a rising tide of patriotic fervor which clamored for war against the "enemies of France."

At the end of June 1899, Pierre Louÿs gave up his bachelor existence and got married. Four months later, Debussy did the same. His bride was a pretty model named Rosalie Texier. Debussy called her Lilly, or Lilly-Lilo. "She's

unbelievably fair, pretty as a picture, and not a bit modern," he wrote to a friend. "Her musical tastes are formed only by her own likes and dislikes. Her favorite song is a round about an old soldier with red cheeks who wears his hat over one ear . . . it's quite awful and not exactly challenging."

Why Debussy married this unsuitable girl is anyone's guess. Probably she reminded him of the pale, fragile Mélisande. The four years or so of their married life were beset by money problems, Lilly's constant illnesses, and the realization that they had nothing at all in common. Nor did she inspire her husband. During this period he produced little music except the suite *Pour le piano* (For the Piano), based on old Baroque forms; and a set of *Estampes* (Prints), also for piano. *Pagodes* (Pagodas) is a delicate picture of the East; *Soirée dans Grenade* (Evening in Granada) a languorous Spanish habañera, while *Jardins sous la pluie* (Gardens in the Rain) is one of his most famous musical impressions.

1897–1899

Debussy with his first wife, Lilly

"Sarabande" from "Pour le piano"

With dignified, stately elegance

6 The Island of Joy

As Queen Victoria's long reign drew to its somber close and the Prince of Wales – who was more at home in the fashionable cafés and nightclubs of Paris than among his straitlaced countrymen – prepared to inaugurate the Edwardian era in England, Paris celebrated the turn of the new century with another extravagant exhibition. This time, the banks of the river Seine were disguised for a whole mile with exotic façades, making the city look like a gigantic film set. Champagne flowed freely, parties lasted until dawn, and in Montmartre and the Latin Quarter on the Left Bank (the traditional haunt of students and down-and-outs), artists tried to outdo each other with ever more outrageous novelties. At Le Lapin Agile (The Lively Bunny), a new Montmartre cabaret which quickly became all the rage, the major attraction was the proprietor's pet donkey, Lolo. A group of young artists persuaded Lolo to "paint" a canvas with his tail, and the resulting work of art, described as an impressionist painting called "And the Sun went Down over the Adriatic" was exhibited at a respectable Paris gallery. Several eminent critics were completely fooled by the hoax.

Debussy, meanwhile, was almost forty years old, and growing tired of living in poverty. His reputation, though, was growing rapidly: within a year of its first performance, *Pelléas et Mélisande* was recognized as a masterpiece, and Debussy unexpectedly found himself famous. In 1903 he was even given an official decoration, as a Chevalier of the Legion of Honor, which he accepted to please his parents.

That autumn, he met Emma Bardac, the wife of a wealthy Jewish banker and a well-known society hostess. Emma, an amateur singer, had already been the mistress of the composer Gabriel Fauré, who dedicated his most famous song-cycle to her, and wrote the charming "Dolly" Suite for her daughter. The same age as Debussy, she was witty, lively, intelligent, and cultured. Debussy fell hopelessly in love with her. In July 1904 he packed Lilly off to her parents in the country, and fled with Emma to the island of Jersey. "The scenery here is marvelous; I'm at peace with myself, and I'm finally free to work, which I haven't been able to do

Debussy with Emma Bardac

31

for a long time," Debussy wrote to his new publisher, Jacques Durand. The first result of this happiness was the exuberant piano piece *L'isle joyeuse* (The Island of Joy). It was inspired by a famous eighteenth-century painting by Watteau showing a group of courtiers and their ladies setting sail for the mythical "island of love," Kythera.

But permanent escape was not possible for the guilty pair. In the autumn they had to return to Paris and face a storm of disapproval. Shortly afterwards Lilly Debussy tried to shoot herself, and the scandal broke in the newspapers. Many of Debussy's old friends, including Pierre Louÿs and the young composer Maurice Ravel (a great admirer of Debussy), took Lilly's side, and set up a fund for the deserted wife. Debussy never forgave them. Despite his social isolation, he was enjoying a more comfortable existence for the first time in his life. He had exchanged his cramped lifestyle in Montmartre for the spacious, upper middle-class elegance

1900-1908

32

of the exclusive Avenue du Bois de Boulogne, near the great park around which the smart carriages of the rich and famous circled each afternoon. The house he and Emma shared was tastefully furnished, with a small garden, a telephone and two servants; and it was there, on October 30, 1905, that their daughter Claude-Emma (known affectionately as "Chou-Chou") was born. Although Debussy's divorce had come through earlier in the year, he did not marry Emma until January 1908.

Debussy's second marriage was by no means smooth sailing. He felt very conscious of the fact that Emma had given up a life of luxury and braved a public scandal for his sake; and for the rest of his life he felt under constant pressure to provide her with an adequate standard of living. Lack of money was still a problem, and he kept falling into debt and having to borrow from moneylenders. In 1907 Emma's wealthy uncle disinherited her; and for the last ten years of his life Debussy was forced to go on concert tours all over Europe, playing the piano and conducting his own works, just to make ends meet. Emma, who was often ill with liver trouble, hated him being away. Debussy was an

Chou-Chou, Debussy and Emma's daughter

The Avenue du Bois de Boulogne, where Debussy and Emma lived

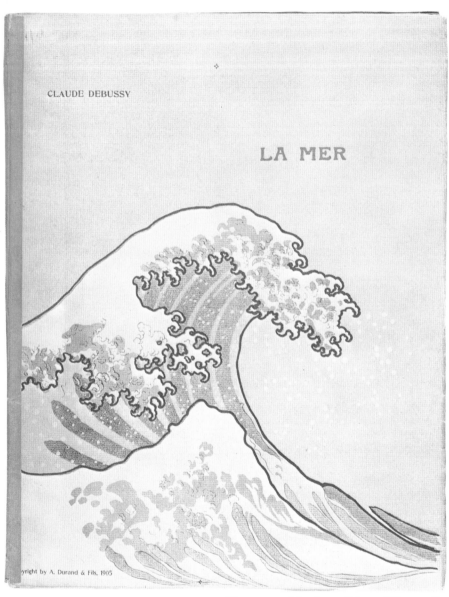

CLAUDE DEBUSSY

LA MER

Copyright by A. Durand & Fils, 1905

The cover of the first edition of "La mer"

attractive man, and Emma was jealous and possessive. Their marriage went through a major crisis around 1910, possibly because Debussy fell in love with another woman. But although he later complained that he and Emma had "lost the ability to enjoy things together," and that he simply was not cut out for domestic life, he was utterly devoted to his small daughter. This time, it would not be so easy to turn his back and walk out. "I promise you, if my little Chou-Chou weren't here I'd blow my head off, silly and ridiculous as that might be," he wrote to his publisher.

In 1905 Debussy took a holiday at Eastbourne, on the Channel coast of England. "It's a charming place," he wrote. "The sea behaves with British politeness . . . What a good place to work! No noise, no pianos, no musicians talking about painting, or painters talking about music." He had just finished one of his most important orchestral pieces, the symphonic poem *La mer* (The Sea). Debussy had never forgotten that his father had wanted him to be a sailor. "I love the sea and have listened to it with the devoted respect it deserves," he wrote. The three movements carry descriptive titles. The first is called "De l'aube à midi sur la mer" (From Dawn to Midday on the Sea) – "I particularly liked the bit at a quarter to eleven," remarked Satie; the second is "Jeux de vagues" (Waves at Play), and the last, "Dialogue du vent et de la mer" (Dialogue Between the Wind and the Sea). This "sea-symphony" is perhaps the most vivid example of Debussy's extraordinary ability to create, through a mosaic of melody and delicate touches of instrumentation, an impression of the ever-shifting, subtle interplay of water and light. "Collect impressions," he advised a pupil. "Don't be in a hurry to write them down. That's something music can do better than painting; it can concentrate variations of color and light in a single frame."

1900-1908

Theme from the last movement of "La mer"

At Eastbourne Debussy also finished a set of three *Images* for piano, entitled *Reflets dans l'eau* (Reflections in Water), *Hommage à Rameau* (Homage to Rameau: a stately dance in grave, eighteenth-century style, recalling one of France's most important composers of the Baroque era), and *Mouvement.* "Without false modesty, I think these three pieces work really well and will take their place in piano literature either to Schumann's right, or Chopin's left," he wrote to his publisher. A second set followed two years later: *Cloches à travers les feuilles* (Bells Through Leaves), *Et la lune descend sur le temple qui fut* (And the Moon Descends on the Temple Which Was: an evocation of a mysterious Oriental landscape), and *Poissons d'or* (Goldfish: said to have been inspired by a piece of Japanese lacquerwork).

Between 1906 and 1908 Debussy wrote mostly piano music. His daughter Chou-Chou had a strict English governess, and Debussy gave mainly English titles to a set of six little piano pieces called *Children's Corner* written for Chou-Chou to play when she got older. Two of them — "Jimbo's Lullaby" and "Serenade for the Doll" — were

The cover of the first edition of "Children's Corner"

A piece of Chinese lacquerwork belonging to Debussy, the inspiration of the piano piece "Poissons d'or"

inspired by Chou-Chou's toys, while in "The Little Shepherd," Debussy may have been thinking of the famous solo for shepherd's pipe which opens the last act of Wagner's opera *Tristan.* At any rate, the last piece, "Golliwogg's Cake-Walk" (based on American ragtime rhythms heard in the Montmartre music halls), pokes fun at Wagner when it suddenly quotes the opening chords from the Prelude to *Tristan. Children's Corner* has ever since been a favorite with young pianists. Debussy, who always took special interest in the presentation of his printed music, instructed his publisher that "the red on the cover should be orange-red — try and give the Golliwogg's head a golden halo, and the cover should be light grey scattered with snow."

36

"Golliwogg's Cake-Walk" from "Children's Corner"

38

7 Invitation to the Dance

By 1909 Debussy was world-famous. *Pelléas* had been performed with outstanding success in Europe and the USA. Though he went to London to supervise the rehearsals for the British premiere, Debussy refused to attend the actual performance, which was wildly applauded. "Such a reaction seems to be very rare in England where the public temperature tends to stay below zero," he commented. He had also begun to accept invitations to conduct his own music. Terrified at first at the prospect of facing "those peculiar beasts called orchestral musicians," Debussy found that he enjoyed the experience of being "the heart of your own music . . . an instrument made up of all possible sound-combinations, let loose just by waving a little stick." To set the seal on his respectability, the venerable Paris Conservatoire finally decided it was time her prodigal son returned, and appointed him a member of its advisory board. Poor Debussy found himself having to sit on juries for the various competitions and prizes. In 1910 he wrote two clarinet pieces for the Conservatoire's annual examinations: *Petite pièce* (Little Piece) for sight-reading and the First Rhapsody as a test-piece.

In 1909 Paris discovered a new craze. The flamboyant impresario Sergey Diaghilev brought his Russian Ballet to town. To the strains of Borodin's vivid *Polovtsian Dances* and Rimsky-Korsakov's exotic *Sheherazade*, conventional ideas about classical ballet were swept aside in a blaze of colorful national costumes, bold stage designs, and daring choreography. Diaghilev, however, was on the lookout for new musical talent, and he approached Debussy. He found the composer deeply depressed. "I'm in the sort of mood where I'd rather be a sponge on the seabed or a vase on the mantelpiece, than a thinking person." He did get as far as

sketching out a scenario for Diaghilev; but then gave it up in favor of finishing his latest orchestral work, a set of three *Images* for orchestra. The second, *Ibéria*, is perhaps the best musical description of Spain by a French composer. Making subtle allusions to Spanish instruments such as the guitar and castanets, it paints a magical picture of a velvety Spanish night, waking to a brilliant fiesta in full sunlight. In contrast, *Rondes de printemps* (Rounds of Spring) uses a wistful little

A design by Bakst for the Russian Ballet production of 'Sheherazade'

Sergey Diaghilev (1872–1929), the Russian impresario

French nursery rhyme to create a mood of childish innocence; while the plaintive Northumbrian folksong "The Keel Row" runs through *Gigues* (finally finished three years later).

Apart from his difficulties with Emma, Debussy's own health was causing trouble. The first symptoms of cancer had appeared, and soon he was forced to take drugs to relieve the pain. As if he knew that time might be short, he began work on the first of two sets of piano pieces – called simply, *Préludes*. These, perhaps his greatest legacy to pianists, sum up his astonishing sympathy for the textures, moods, and sounds a piano can make, without resorting to an overpowering virtuosity. Each piece has a descriptive title, such as *Des pas sur la neige* (Footsteps in the Snow), *Danseuses de Delphes* (Delphic Dancers), or *Les collines d'Anacapri* (The Hills of Anacapri), but Debussy insisted that they should appear only at the end, so as not to prejudice the player. Of the two most famous pieces in Book One, one is *La cathédrale engloutie* (The Submerged Cathedral), inspired by an old Breton legend of a drowned city which rises once a year from the waves. Here massive clusters of chords evoke the tolling of distant bells, until the great cathedral "emerges gradually from the haze," and then sinks back beneath the sea. The other is a charming, simple portrait of a country girl "with flaxen hair": *La fille aux cheveux de lin*. Three years later, Debussy added a second set of Préludes, in which mood-paintings mingle with exotic landscapes, and character sketches provide a touch of quirky humor.

1909–1913

"La fille aux cheveux de lin" from "Préludes," Book I

In 1910 Debussy went on a conducting tour to Vienna and Budapest. It was a great success, but Debussy felt he was not cut out to be "the composer abroad" – it made him feel like a commercial traveller. "Once there was a daddy who lived in exile . . . and every day he missed his little Chou-Chou," he wrote touchingly to his daughter. A Hungarian journalist who interviewed him found a "friendly and rather nervy Frenchman. He's not old, just forty-eight, but looks younger, with his hair and dark beard. His curly hair, dark complexion and flattened nose make him look like a negro. He has an attractive face, velvety eyes, and a deep, gentle voice. Sometimes he looks like a satisfied faun, sometimes like a naïve child."

On the beach at Houlgate with Chou-Chou, 1911

Debussy in 1909

The next year, Debussy finally ventured into ballet music. Rather reluctantly, he accepted a commission from the Canadian dancer Maud Allan for an exotic "Egyptian" ballet called *Khamma*. "The plot could have been written by a baby – it's of no interest at all," wrote Debussy. Nor is the music up to his usual standard. At the same time he was approached by the poet and playwright Gabriele d'Annunzio, who wanted some incidental music for a play based on the martyrdom of St. Sebastian. The part of the Saint – who comes to a grisly end under a hail of arrows – was danced by the eccentric Ida Rubinstein (who was only too eager to show off her famously long legs). Not surprisingly, the play's rather dubious mixture of sex and religion caused a scandal: the Archbishop of Paris promptly forbade all good Catholics to go and see it, and though Debussy claimed that his music was "quite suitable for a church," it was a flop.

Not until 1912 did Debussy take up Diaghilev's invitation to write for the Russian Ballet. Its brilliant star dancer

A poster advertising Nijinsky in the ballet "L'après-midi d'un faune"

42

Nijinsky – a "young savage . . . who adds up demisemiquavers with his feet" – was interested in choreographing some of Debussy's orchestral works, including *L'après-midi d'un faune*. Produced as a ballet in 1912, Nijinsky's suggestive treatment of Debussy's music annoyed the composer and provoked a great deal of criticism. At the same time, Nijinsky persuaded Debussy to start work on a new ballet. Its subject was the tantalizing relationship between two girls and a young man playing a game of tennis on a warm, sultry evening. *Jeux* (Games), a web of sound in which fragments of melodies emerge and disappear in response to the players' useless search for their lost tennis ball, and their brief, flirtatious scufflings, is now considered a masterpiece of twentieth-century music. But it was not much appreciated at its first performance on May 15, 1913. In fact, it was quickly overshadowed by the notorious première of Stravinsky's *Rite of Spring* two weeks later, amid one of the celebrated Parisian theatrical riots, in which audiences hissed, jeered, and threw objects at the performers. Debussy, who had known Stravinsky for three years, and had given him much help and encouragement, acknowledged that it was now up to the talented young Russian to "enlarge the boundaries of what is possible in the kingdom of sound." As for Stravinsky, he and other composers of his generation freely acknowledged that they "owed the most to Debussy."

Igor Stravinsky
(1882–1971)

1909-1913

An original design for the
Russian Ballet production of "Jeux"

*Fashionable Paris in 1913:
the rue de la Paix*

1914-1918

8 "Musicien français"

As the fateful year 1914 approached, the great powers eyed each other with increasing suspicion, while making secret deals and privately rushing to build up their armies. The last surviving rulers of ancient dynasties struggled to cling on to the rags of power, while under the glittering chandeliers of sumptuous ballrooms from London to St. Petersburg, a doomed generation danced its way headlong to disaster. In 1912 the "unsinkable" luxury liner *Titanic* – a miracle of engineering – hit an iceberg on her maiden voyage across the Atlantic and sank, drowning millionaires and poor immigrants alike and shattering men's faith in up-to-date technology. Meanwhile, as Europe marched inexorably towards the brink of war, the arts continued to blossom in Paris. Styles came and went in headlong succession – post-impressionism gave way to Picasso's disjointed "cubism," new theaters opened with avant-garde plays, "futurism" was the buzzword, and the novels of Proust and James Joyce began to appear in print. Erik Satie emerged from twelve silent years of exile in a dreary working-class suburb of Paris, to find –

much to his astonishment – his eccentric music in demand. Debussy, however, felt isolated, cut off from many of his old friends, and painfully aware that he was no longer at the forefront of new ideas. As his illness took hold, he became increasingly worried about the state of French music. "There's too much German influence in France, and we're still stifled by it . . . Wagner's ideas have had a bad influence on much music and many countries," he wrote in 1910. That year, he finished two sets of songs. These drew fresh inspiration from the past, especially the riotous atmosphere of medieval Paris conjured up in the lively verses of François Villon, the fifteenth-century poet and murderer who twice escaped the gallows.

The outbreak of the First World War in August 1914 revived all Debussy's childhood memories and fears. "The military mentality doesn't suit me at all; I've never had to handle a gun," he wrote to his publisher. Nevertheless he felt ashamed that he was doing nothing to support the war effort, and when the British *Daily Telegraph* organized a tribute to the courage of the Belgians (then in the front line), Debussy – along with several other British and French composers – was quick to contribute a little *Berceuse héroïque* (Heroic Lullaby) for piano. "French art needs to take its revenge quite as much as the French army does," he wrote. His own music was certainly seeking new directions.

Encouraged by his studies of eighteenth-century French music, before the time when German ideals took over and swamped France's native culture, Debussy gradually abandoned the sensuous harmonies of his own impressionist period, in favor of a more austere, unemotional approach, based on the "profound grace" of the old harpsichordists.

"Berceuse héroïque"

A First World War battlefield, 1917

Debussy and Emma spent the summer of 1915 at Pourville, on the Channel coast. There, he worked feverishly, in "secret homage" to the young men of France, mown down in the thousands on the battlefields. His publisher had asked him to edit the complete piano works of Chopin, and while he found the task terrifying, Chopin's music inspired him to complete his last major piano work, two sets of brilliant studies, each of which develops a particular point of technique. Debussy's *Études* are now rated by pianists alongside Chopin's. He also finished three equally "abstract" pieces for two pianos, called – appropriately – *En blanc et noir* (In White and Black), one of which is dedicated to a friend who had been killed in action.

At the same time he began work on a set of sonatas – his first important chamber music since the String Quartet of twenty years earlier. "There will be six, for different instrumental groups, and the last will combine all the instruments from the previous five," he told a friend. By the autumn he had completed the first two "in the old, flexible style." The Cello Sonata makes little use of the cello's singing tone: instead it is a quirky, nervous dialogue which Debussy called "Pierrot fâché avec la lune" (Pierrot Angry With the Moon). In some ways it represents Debussy's own disenchantment with the distant, pre-war world of moonlit serenades and lovers' meetings he had once created. The Sonata for flute, viola, and harp is more exquisite in sound and texture. "It dates from a time when I was still in touch with music . . . a memory of a Debussy of long ago," said the composer; but he felt it was so sad he was unsure whether it should make people laugh or cry.

On returning to Paris, Debussy faced an operation for his fast-growing cancer. He survived, but for the rest of his life he was in great pain. Although he continued to work on

Debussy with Chou-Chou at Le Moulleau, 1916

his great opera project, *La chute de la maison Usher* (The Fall of the House of Usher), which had haunted him for nearly ten years, he only managed to complete one more piece, the third of his planned set of six sonatas. Debussy played the piano at the first performance of the Violin Sonata in Paris in May 1917, and once again in the autumn. That was his last public appearance.

Meanwhile, the war ground on, inflicting terrible suffering on everyone involved. In early 1918 the last great German offensive began, and by the end of March, Paris was pounded by enemy bombs and artillery. By then, Debussy was bedridden, too weak to be taken down to the cellar. On the evening of March 25, Chou-Chou was called to her father's side. "I thought it was all over," she later told her half-brother. "But when I went back, Daddy was asleep, breathing regularly but gently. He slept like that until ten o'clock in the evening, and then, quietly, like an angel, he went to sleep for ever . . . It's dreadful. I don't know how to go on living, and I can't believe it's true." (Poor little Chou-Chou did not survive her father by very long: she died of diphtheria just sixteen months later, aged thirteen.)

Debussy was only fifty-five when he died. He never finished his set of sonatas; but the three that were published carry a simple inscription which sums up his achievement – "Claude Debussy: French musician."

List of Works

Debussy left many pieces unfinished, or only sketched out. These are his most important works:

Operas

Pelléas et Mélisande (1893–1902); 3 unfinished: *Rodrigue et Chimène* (1890–2); *Le diable dans le beffroi* (The Devil in the Belfry, 1902–11); *La chute de la maison Usher* (1908–17).

Ballets

Khamma (1911–12); *Jeux* (1912–13); *La boîte à joujoux* (The Box of Playthings) (children's ballet, incomplete, 1913).

Incidental music

Le roi Lear (King Lear, incomplete, 1904); *Le martyre de Saint-Sébastien* (1911).

Orchestral

Printemps (symphonic suite, 1887); Fantaisie for piano and orchestra (1889–90); *Prélude à l'après-midi d'un faune* (1892–4); Nocturnes (1897–9); *La mer* (3 symphonic sketches, 1903–5); *Danse sacrée et danse profane* (for chromatic harp and strings, 1904); *Images* (1905– 12).

Voice and orchestra

L'enfant prodigue (1884); *La damoiselle élue* (1887–8).

Choral

3 Songs of Charles d'Orléans (1898).

Chamber Music

String Quartet (1893); Rhapsody for alto saxophone and piano (1901–8); First Rhapsody for clarinet and piano (1909–10); Little Piece for clarinet and piano (1910); Syrinx for flute (1913); Cello Sonata (1915); Sonata for flute, viola and harp (1915); Violin Sonata (1916–17).

Songs

Around 85, including *Ariettes, paysages belges et aquarelles* (Verlaine, 1888); 5 Poems of Baudelaire (1887–89); 3 Songs (Verlaine, 1891); *Fêtes galantes* (Verlaine; set 1, 1891; set 2, 1904); *Proses lyriques* (Debussy, 1892–3); *Chansons de Bilitis* (Louÿs, 1897–8); 3 Songs of France (1904); *Le promenoir des deux amants* (Tristan l'Hermite, 1904–10); 3 Ballades of Villon (François Villon, 1910); 3 Poems of Mallarmé (1913).

Piano

2 Arabesques (1888–91); *Suite bergamasque* (1890); *Pour le piano* (1894–1901); *Estampes* (1903); *L'isle joyeuse* (1904); *Images*, set 1 (1905); set 2 (1907); *Children's Corner* (1906–8); *Hommage à Haydn* (1909); *Le petit nègre* (The little Negro, 1909); *Préludes*, Book 1 (1909–10); Book 2 (1912–13); *Berceuse héroïque* (1914); *Études* (1915).
Petite Suite (piano duet, 1886–9); 6 *Epigraphes Antiques* (piano duet, 1914); *En blanc et noir* (2 pianos, 1915).

Picture Credits

The author and publishers have made every effort to identify the owners of the pictures used in this publication; they apologize for any inaccuracies and would like to thank the following:
(*a, b* and *c* indicate left to right/top to bottom)

Mary Evans Picture Library 2, 4c, 8b, 13a, 14a, 16b, 18b, 28, 31a, 32a, 33, 44.
Reproduced by kind permission of The Witch Ball 3c, 6b, 9a, 16a, 17, 24b.
ET Archive 42b, 43b, 46.
John Massey Stewart 4a, 39a.
Sally Gould (photos) 5a, 9c.
Musée de Petit Palais 7a.
Musée du Louvre, Paris 15b, 22.
Museum of Albi 18a.
Musée des Beaux-Arts, Rouen 27.
Publisher's collection 3a, 3b, 9b, 10, 24a, 25a, 25b.
Author's collection 36b, 43a.

The cover shows a portrait of Debussy in 1884 by Baschat against the Eiffel Tower illuminated for the 1889 Exhibition and the Olympia Music Hall, Paris (Mary Evans Picture Library).

The author wishes to acknowledge her debt to many sources, including Edward Lockspeiser: *Debussy: His Life and Mind* (London, 1962); Léon Vallas: *Claude Debussy: His Life and Works* (London, 1933); Roger Nichols: *Debussy* (Grove 6) and François Lesure and Roger Nichols, eds: *Debussy Letters* (London, 1988). She also wishes to thank Richard King, editor of the *Composer's World* series, for his invaluable help with the text and with picture research.

VIKING
Published by the Penguin Group
Penguin Books USA Inc., 375 Hudson Street, New York, New York 10014, U.S.A.
Penguin Books Ltd, 27 Wrights Lane, London W8 5TZ, England
Penguin Books Australia Ltd, Ringwood, Victoria, Australia
Penguin Books Canada Ltd, 10 Alcorn Avenue, Toronto, Ontario, Canada M4V 3B2
Penguin Books (N.Z.) Ltd, 182–190 Wairau Road, Auckland 10, New Zealand

Penguin Books Ltd, Registered Offices: Harmondsworth, Middlesex, England

First published in Great Britain in 1993 by Faber Music Ltd in association with Faber and Faber Ltd

First published in the United States of America in 1993 by Viking, a division of Penguin Books USA Inc.

10 9 8 7 6 5 4 3 2 1

Library of Congress Catalog Card Number: 92–85504

ISBN 0-670-84482-9

Printed in Spain by Mateu Cromo, Madrid

Set in Sabon Roman